THE ANXIETY ANTIDOTE: PRACTICAL STRATEGIES FOR FINDING PEACE AND CALM

A Practical Guide to Finding Freedom from Worry and Stress

Asa Eccleston Kibilski

CONTENTS

UNDERSTANDING ANXIETY

What is Anxiety?

Picture this: You're getting ready for a big presentation at work. Your heart pounds in your chest like a drum solo. Your palms sweat, leaving damp fingerprints on your carefully prepared notes. Your mind races, jumping from one worst-case scenario to the next. You feel an overwhelming sense of dread, as if something terrible is about to happen.

Sound familiar? If so, you're not alone. Millions of people around the world experience anxiety every day. It's a normal human emotion, a natural response to stress or danger. But for some, anxiety becomes overwhelming, interfering with daily life and causing significant distress.

So, what exactly is anxiety? At its core, anxiety is your body's alarm system, designed to protect you from harm. It's that fight-or-flight response that kicks in when you face a threat, real or perceived. Think of it as your internal security guard, constantly scanning the environment for potential dangers and sounding the alarm when it senses something amiss.

When you're anxious, your body releases stress hormones like adrenaline and cortisol. These hormones trigger a cascade of physical changes, preparing you to either fight the threat or flee from it. Your heart rate and breathing increase, your muscles tense, and your senses sharpen. All of this happens in an instant, without you even having to think about it.

But anxiety isn't just a physical experience. It also affects your thoughts and feelings. You may find yourself worrying excessively, dwelling on negative possibilities, and struggling to concentrate. You may feel restless, irritable, or on edge. In severe cases, anxiety can lead to panic attacks, characterized by intense fear, rapid heartbeat, and shortness of breath.

What's important to understand is that anxiety exists on a spectrum. We all experience it to some degree, and it's perfectly normal to feel anxious from time to time. But when anxiety becomes persistent, excessive, and out of proportion to the actual threat, it can be a sign of an anxiety disorder.

Anxiety disorders are the most common mental illness in the world, affecting millions of people. There are different types of anxiety disorders, each with its own unique set of symptoms. Some of the most common include generalized anxiety disorder (GAD), panic disorder, social anxiety disorder, and specific phobias.

While the exact causes of anxiety disorders are unknown, scientists believe that a combination of genetic, environmental, and psychological factors play a role. Some people may be more genetically predisposed to anxiety, while others may develop anxiety disorders as a result of stressful life events or trauma.

The good news is that anxiety is treatable. With the right tools and support, you can learn to manage your anxiety and regain control of your life.

The Different Faces of Anxiety

Anxiety isn't a one-size-fits-all experience. It can manifest in a multitude of ways, each with its own unique set of symptoms and challenges. Think of anxiety as a chameleon, blending into the background of your life but changing its colors depending on the situation.

For some, anxiety is a constant companion, a low-level hum of worry that buzzes in the background of their thoughts. They may find it difficult to relax, constantly on edge, and always anticipating the worst. This is often the case with Generalized Anxiety Disorder (GAD), where worry becomes pervasive and difficult to control.

For others, anxiety strikes suddenly and intensely, like a lightning bolt out of the blue. These are panic attacks, episodes of overwhelming fear that can feel like a heart attack. The world seems to close in, your heart races, you struggle to breathe, and a sense of impending doom washes over you. Panic disorder is characterized by these recurring panic attacks, often accompanied by a fear of having another attack.

Social anxiety disorder (SAD) is another common form of anxiety. It's a deep-seated fear of social situations, where you may feel judged, embarrassed, or humiliated. Simple tasks like making a phone call, attending a party, or speaking in public can become insurmountable challenges. You may avoid social interactions altogether, leading to isolation and loneliness.

Then there are specific phobias, intense fears of specific objects or situations. It could be a fear of spiders, heights, flying, or even something as seemingly harmless as clowns. These phobias can be incredibly debilitating, causing you to avoid the things you fear and limiting your life in significant ways.

Anxiety can also show up in more subtle ways. You may find yourself procrastinating, unable to make decisions, or constantly second-guessing yourself. You may experience physical symptoms like stomach aches, headaches, or muscle tension. You may have trouble sleeping or find yourself overly irritable or easily angered.

It's important to recognize that anxiety can look different for everyone. What triggers one person may not trigger another. The severity of symptoms can also vary widely. Some people experience mild anxiety that comes and goes, while others struggle with debilitating anxiety that interferes with their daily lives.

The good news is that no matter what form your anxiety takes, there are effective treatments available. By understanding the different faces of anxiety, you can learn to recognize your own unique triggers and symptoms, and develop coping strategies that work for you.

THE MIND-BODY CONNECTION

How Anxiety Affects the Body

Have you ever noticed how your stomach churns before a big test? Or how your heart races when you're about to give a presentation? Maybe you've even experienced a headache so intense it feels like a vice grip on your skull during a stressful week. These aren't mere coincidences; they're your body's way of screaming, "I'm anxious!"

Anxiety isn't just a feeling – it's a full-body experience. It's your mind and body working in tandem, a symphony of stress that can leave you feeling physically and emotionally drained. But why does this happen? Let's dive into the fascinating science behind the mind-body connection.

When you encounter a threat – whether it's a snarling dog or a looming deadline – your brain's alarm system, the amygdala, sends out an SOS. This triggers a cascade of reactions, flooding your body with stress hormones like adrenaline and cortisol. These hormones are like the body's Red Bull, giving you a temporary energy boost to fight or flee from danger.

In the short term, this stress response can be helpful, providing the focus and strength you need to tackle a challenge. But when anxiety becomes chronic, these stress hormones can wreak havoc on your body.

Your heart may start pounding like a bass drum, your breathing may become shallow and rapid, and your muscles may tense up like coiled springs. These are all classic signs of the fight-or-flight response. You might also experience dizziness, nausea, or a churning stomach – all thanks to the adrenaline coursing through your veins.

But anxiety's effects go beyond these immediate physical symptoms. Chronic stress can weaken your immune system, making you more susceptible to colds, infections, and other illnesses. It can also disrupt your sleep, leaving you feeling tired and irritable. Over time, chronic anxiety has been linked to more serious health problems, including heart disease, high blood pressure, and digestive issues.

And it doesn't stop there. Anxiety can also affect your brain, impairing your memory, concentration, and decision-making abilities. It can make it difficult to focus on tasks, remember important information, and think clearly. This is because chronic stress can actually shrink the hippocampus, a part of the brain responsible for learning and memory.

So, the next time you feel that knot in your stomach or that tension in your shoulders, remember that it's not just "all in your head." Anxiety is a real, physical experience that can have a profound impact on your body and brain.

The good news is that by understanding the mind-body connection, you can learn to recognize the signs of anxiety and develop strategies to manage it. By addressing both the physical and mental aspects of anxiety, you can break free from its grip and reclaim your well-being.

The Role of Stress Hormones

Imagine your body as a finely tuned orchestra, each instrument playing its part to create a harmonious melody. Now, picture anxiety as a rogue conductor, waving its baton frantically and throwing the entire symphony into disarray.

The culprits behind this chaos? Stress hormones. These chemical messengers, primarily adrenaline and cortisol, are like the body's emergency responders, rushing to the scene when danger is detected. But when anxiety becomes a chronic condition, these hormones can overstay their welcome, turning a helpful alarm system into a cacophony of stress.

Adrenaline, also known as epinephrine, is the body's "get up and go" hormone. It's responsible for the rapid heartbeat, quickened breathing, and surge of energy you feel when faced with a threat. It's what gives you the strength to lift a car off a trapped loved one or sprint away from danger. But when anxiety keeps your adrenaline levels chronically elevated, it can leave you feeling constantly on edge, jittery, and unable to relax.

Cortisol, on the other hand, is the body's "long-haul" stress hormone. It helps regulate your metabolism, immune response, and even your sleep-wake cycle. In small doses, cortisol is essential for survival. But when anxiety keeps your cortisol levels high, it can disrupt these essential functions, leading to fatigue, insomnia, weight gain, and even a weakened immune system.

Think of it like this: Imagine your stress hormones as a car's accelerator. In small doses, they help you get where you need to go quickly. But if you keep your foot on the gas pedal for too long, you'll burn out the engine.

The long-term effects of chronic stress hormone exposure can be serious. It can increase your risk of developing heart disease, high blood pressure, diabetes, and even depression. It can also impair your cognitive function, making it harder to concentrate, remember things, and make decisions.

But here's the good news: You're not at the mercy of your stress hormones. By understanding how they work, you can learn to manage their effects and restore harmony to your body's orchestra.

IDENTIFYING YOUR TRIGGERS

Common Anxiety Triggers

Imagine your anxiety as a slumbering dragon, curled up deep within you. Most of the time, it's dormant, but certain things can awaken it, causing it to stir and breathe fire into your life. These things are known as triggers, and they can vary widely from person to person.

For some, it's the mundane tasks of daily life: a traffic jam, a crowded elevator, a stack of unpaid bills. For others, it's major life events: a job interview, a wedding, a medical diagnosis. And for many, it's the relentless pressure of social media, constantly comparing themselves to others and feeling like they're falling short.

But anxiety triggers aren't always external. Sometimes, they come from within. It could be a nagging worry about the future, a painful memory from the past, or a deep-seated insecurity. It could even be something as seemingly innocuous as a racing heartbeat or a slight tremor in your hand.

Think of your triggers as breadcrumbs, leading you to the source of your anxiety. By identifying these triggers, you can start to understand what sets off your anxiety and develop strategies to manage it.

Here are some of the most common anxiety triggers:

- **Social situations:** Parties, public speaking, meeting new people, or even just having a casual conversation can be anxiety-inducing for some.
- **Performance anxiety:** The pressure to perform well at work,

school, or in sports can trigger anxiety in many people.

- **Health concerns:** Worrying about your health or the health of loved ones can be a major source of anxiety.
- **Financial worries:** Money troubles, debt, and job insecurity can all contribute to anxiety.
- **Relationship problems:** Conflicts with friends, family, or romantic partners can trigger anxiety.
- **Major life changes:** Moving, starting a new job, or getting married can all be stressful and anxiety-provoking.
- **World events:** News of natural disasters, political unrest, or economic instability can cause anxiety in many people.

But it's important to remember that these are just a few examples. Your triggers may be different, and that's okay. The key is to be aware of what sets off your anxiety so you can learn to manage it.

Identifying your triggers is like finding the pieces of a puzzle. Each trigger is a clue that can help you understand the bigger picture of your anxiety. By piecing together these clues, you can start to see the patterns and connections that underlie your anxiety and develop a personalized plan to manage it.

Tracking Your Anxiety Patterns

Imagine you're a detective, hot on the trail of a mysterious culprit. Your mission: to uncover the secrets of your anxiety. And your most valuable tool? A simple notebook.

Tracking your anxiety patterns is like keeping a diary of your emotional landscape. It's a way to document the ups and downs of your anxiety, identify triggers, and monitor the effectiveness of your coping strategies. By becoming a keen observer of your own experience, you can gain valuable insights into what makes your anxiety tick.

Think of your anxiety tracker as a treasure map, guiding you toward the hidden gems of self-awareness. It's a way to connect the dots between your thoughts, feelings, and behaviors, and to understand how they contribute to your anxiety.

Here's how you can start tracking your anxiety patterns:

1. **Choose a format:** You can use a traditional notebook, a smartphone app, or even a spreadsheet. The important thing is to choose a format that works for you and that you'll be consistent with.
2. **Record your anxiety levels:** Throughout the day, take a few moments to check in with yourself and rate your anxiety on a scale of 1 to 10. Note any physical symptoms you're experiencing, such as a racing heart, sweaty palms, or a knot in your stomach.
3. **Identify triggers:** What were you doing or thinking about when your anxiety spiked? Were you in a social situation, facing a deadline, or having a difficult conversation?
4. **Note your coping strategies:** What did you do to manage your anxiety? Did you take deep breaths, practice mindfulness, or talk to a friend?
5. **Track your progress:** Over time, you'll start to see patterns emerge. You'll notice which situations tend to trigger your anxiety, which coping strategies are most effective, and how your anxiety levels fluctuate throughout the day.

This information is like gold for your anxiety-fighting arsenal. It can help you anticipate triggers, develop a personalized toolkit of coping skills, and track your progress over time. It can also be invaluable information to share with your therapist or doctor, helping them tailor a treatment plan that meets your specific needs.

Remember, tracking your anxiety patterns isn't about judgment or criticism. It's about self-discovery and empowerment. By understanding your anxiety, you can learn to manage it and live a fuller, more fulfilling life.

MINDFULNESS AND MEDITATION

The Basics of Mindfulness

Imagine your mind as a bustling marketplace, filled with the chatter of competing thoughts, worries, and anxieties. It's a chaotic scene, with vendors hawking their wares, children clamoring for attention, and merchants haggling over prices. In the midst of this chaos, mindfulness is your quiet sanctuary, a tranquil oasis where you can escape the noise and find inner peace.

Mindfulness is the practice of paying attention to the present moment without judgment. It's about being fully engaged in whatever you're doing, whether it's washing dishes, walking the dog, or simply breathing. It's about noticing the sights, sounds, smells, and sensations around you, and accepting them without trying to change them.

Think of mindfulness as a magnifying glass, focusing your attention on the here and now. It's a way to slow down, tune into your body and mind, and cultivate a sense of awareness and acceptance.

But mindfulness isn't just about zoning out or ignoring your problems. It's about facing them head-on, but with a sense of curiosity and compassion. It's about acknowledging your thoughts and feelings without getting caught up in them. It's about recognizing that you are not your thoughts, but rather the observer of your thoughts.

So how do you practice mindfulness? It's simpler than you might think. Start by finding a quiet place where you won't be disturbed.

Sit comfortably, either on a chair or on the floor. Close your eyes or soften your gaze. Then, bring your attention to your breath. Notice the rise and fall of your chest, the sensation of air flowing in and out of your nostrils.

If your mind starts to wander – and it will – gently bring it back to your breath. Don't judge yourself for getting distracted. It's a natural part of the process. Simply acknowledge the thought and let it go, returning your focus to your breath.

You can also practice mindfulness during everyday activities. While you're eating, pay attention to the taste, texture, and aroma of your food. While you're walking, notice the sensation of your feet hitting the ground, the wind on your skin, and the sounds around you.

The key is to be present, engaged, and non-judgmental. Accept whatever arises in your awareness, whether it's pleasant or unpleasant. Remember, mindfulness isn't about emptying your mind or achieving a state of bliss. It's about being fully present in the moment, with all of its ups and downs.

With regular practice, mindfulness can help you reduce stress, improve your mood, and increase your self-awareness. It can also help you manage anxiety by teaching you to observe your thoughts and feelings without getting caught up in them.

Mindfulness Exercises for Anxiety

Imagine you're standing at the edge of a turbulent ocean. Waves of anxiety crash against you, threatening to pull you under. But you have a life raft: mindfulness exercises. These simple practices are like anchors, grounding you in the present moment and helping you ride out the storm.

Mindfulness exercises are tools you can use to cultivate awareness, focus, and calm. They can help you break free from the grip of anxiety by teaching you to observe your thoughts and feelings without judgment. They can also help you develop a sense of inner peace and resilience, so you can face life's challenges with greater ease.

Here are a few mindfulness exercises you can try:

1. **Body Scan Meditation:** Lie down or sit comfortably. Close your eyes and take a few deep breaths. Then, slowly bring your attention to each part of your body, starting with your toes and working your way up to your head. Notice any sensations you feel, such as warmth, tingling, or tightness. If your mind wanders, gently bring it back to your body.
pen_spark

2. **Mindful Breathing:** Sit in a comfortable position and close your eyes. Bring your attention to your breath. Notice the rise and fall of your chest, the sensation of air flowing in and out of your nostrils. If your mind starts to wander, gently bring it back to your breath. Count each breath, if that helps you focus.

3. **Mindful Walking:** Go for a walk in a quiet place. As you walk, pay attention to the sensation of your feet hitting the ground, the movement of your legs, and the feeling of the air on your skin. Notice the sights, sounds, and smells around you.

4. **Mindful Eating:** Choose a small piece of food, such as a raisin or a piece of chocolate. Examine it closely, noticing its color, texture, and shape. Then, slowly put it in your mouth and savor the taste, noticing the different flavors and sensations.

5. **Loving-Kindness Meditation:** Sit comfortably and close your eyes. Bring to mind someone you love and wish them well. Then, extend that feeling of love and kindness to yourself, to someone you feel neutral about, and even to someone you find difficult. Repeat phrases like "May you be happy," "May you be healthy," and "May you be at peace."

Remember, mindfulness exercises are like any other skill – they take practice. Don't get discouraged if your mind wanders or you find it difficult to focus at first. Just keep practicing, and eventually, you'll start to see the benefits.

With regular practice, mindfulness exercises can help you reduce anxiety, improve your mood, and increase your self-awareness. They can also help you develop a sense of inner peace and resilience, so you can face life's challenges with greater ease and grace.

BREATHING TECHNIQUES

The Power of Breath

Imagine you're holding a balloon. As you inhale, the balloon expands, filling with air. As you exhale, it deflates, releasing the air back into the world. Now, imagine that balloon is your own body, and the air is your breath. With each inhale, you're filling yourself with life-giving oxygen, nourishing your body and calming your mind. With each exhale, you're releasing tension and stress, letting go of what no longer serves you.

Breath is the foundation of life, the rhythm that connects us to our bodies and to the world around us. It's a powerful tool for managing anxiety, a natural tranquilizer that we carry with us wherever we go. Yet, in the midst of our busy lives, we often forget to breathe consciously, taking shallow, hurried breaths that only fuel our anxiety.

But when you learn to harness the power of your breath, you can tap into a wellspring of calm and clarity. You can soothe your nervous system, quiet your racing mind, and restore balance to your body.

Breathing techniques are like a secret weapon in the fight against anxiety. They're simple, accessible, and incredibly effective. And the best part? They're always available to you, no matter where you are or what you're doing.

But how does breathing work to calm anxiety? It all comes down to the autonomic nervous system, the control center for your body's involuntary functions like heart rate, digestion, and breathing. This system has two branches: the sympathetic nervous system, which revs you up for action, and the parasympathetic nervous system, which calms you down and promotes rest and relaxation.

When you're anxious, your sympathetic nervous system is in overdrive, flooding your body with stress hormones and triggering the fight-or-flight response. But by slowing down your breath and breathing deeply, you can activate your parasympathetic nervous system, sending a signal to your body that it's safe to relax.

This is why breathing techniques are so effective for managing anxiety. They give you a way to take control of your nervous system and shift it from a state of stress to a state of calm.

So, the next time you feel anxiety creeping in, take a moment to pause and breathe. Feel the rise and fall of your chest, the sensation of air flowing in and out of your nostrils. Let your breath be your anchor, grounding you in the present moment and reminding you that you are safe and in control.

Breathing Exercises for Calm

Imagine your breath as a gentle breeze, capable of soothing your frayed nerves and calming your racing mind. It's more than just inhaling and exhaling; it's a rhythmic dance that can harmonize your body and mind, restoring a sense of peace and tranquility.

Breathing exercises aren't just ancient wisdom or New Age fads; they're backed by a growing body of scientific evidence. Studies have shown that specific breathing techniques can trigger the relaxation response, a physiological state characterized by lowered heart rate, blood pressure, and muscle tension. This isn't just about feeling calmer; it's about tangible changes in your body's chemistry.

One such technique is diaphragmatic breathing, also known as belly breathing. It involves inhaling deeply through your nose, allowing your belly to expand while your chest remains relatively still. As you exhale slowly through your mouth, your belly contracts. This type of breathing activates the vagus nerve, a major player in the parasympathetic nervous system, which is responsible for rest and digest functions. Research has shown that diaphragmatic breathing can reduce cortisol levels, the stress hormone, and increase heart rate variability, a marker of a healthy nervous system.

Another effective technique is box breathing, also known as four-square breathing. It involves inhaling for a count of four, holding your breath for a count of four, exhaling for a count of four, and holding your breath again for a count of four. This rhythmic pattern helps to regulate your breath and slow down your heart rate. A study published in the Journal of Alternative and Complementary Medicine found that box breathing can significantly reduce anxiety and improve mood in just a few minutes.

Alternate nostril breathing, a yogic practice known as nadi shodhana, is another powerful tool. It involves closing one nostril while inhaling through the other, then closing the opposite nostril while exhaling. This technique is believed to balance the two hemispheres of the brain and promote a sense of calm. Research has shown that alternate nostril breathing can reduce stress, improve cognitive function, and even enhance creativity.

The beauty of these breathing exercises is their simplicity. You don't need any special equipment or training, just a quiet place and a few minutes of your time. You can practice them anywhere, anytime – at your desk, in the car, or even in line at the grocery store.

By incorporating these techniques into your daily routine, you can build resilience to stress and cultivate a sense of inner peace. Remember, your breath is always with you, a constant companion that can guide you back to calm whenever anxiety threatens to take over.

COGNITIVE RESTRUCTURING

Identifying Negative Thought Patterns

Imagine your mind as a movie theater, and your thoughts as the film playing on the screen. Now, picture that film constantly showing scenes of impending doom, failure, and rejection. It's a bleak picture, isn't it? This is the reality for many people struggling with anxiety, their minds trapped in a loop of negative thoughts and beliefs.

These negative thought patterns are like distorted lenses, warping your perception of reality and amplifying your fears. They can convince you that you're not good enough, that you're going to fail, or that something terrible is about to happen. And the more you believe these thoughts, the more anxious you become.

But here's the thing: You're not a helpless audience member, forced to watch this negative film on repeat. You have the power to change the channel, to rewrite the script, and to create a more positive and empowering narrative.

Identifying these negative thought patterns is the first step towards cognitive restructuring, a powerful technique for managing anxiety. It's like shining a spotlight on the dark corners of your mind, exposing the distorted thoughts that fuel your fears.

These negative thoughts often fall into certain categories:

- **Catastrophizing:** Imagining the worst-case scenario and blowing things out of proportion. For example, thinking you'll lose your job because you made a minor mistake.
- **All-or-nothing thinking:** Seeing things in black and white

terms, with no middle ground. For example, believing you're a total failure if you don't get a perfect score on a test.

- **Mind reading:** Assuming you know what others are thinking, usually in a negative way. For example, believing your friends are secretly judging you.
- **Fortune telling:** Predicting the future, often with negative outcomes. For example, believing you'll never find love or success.
- **Personalization:** Taking everything personally and blaming yourself for things that are outside of your control. For example, feeling responsible for a friend's bad mood.

These negative thought patterns are like weeds in a garden, choking out the positive thoughts and beliefs that can nourish your mental well-being. But by identifying these weeds, you can start to pull them out and replace them with healthier, more realistic thoughts.

The next time you notice yourself feeling anxious, take a moment to pause and examine your thoughts. Are you catastrophizing? Engaging in all-or-nothing thinking? Mind reading? Fortune telling? Personalizing? By becoming aware of these negative thought patterns, you can start to challenge them and replace them with more positive, empowering beliefs.

Challenging and Replacing Anxious Thoughts

Imagine you're a lawyer, standing before a jury, defending your client against a barrage of accusations. The prosecutor, in this case, is your own anxious mind, hurling distorted thoughts and irrational fears at you. But you're not going to let these accusations stand unchallenged. You're going to cross-examine them, expose their flaws, and present a more balanced and accurate picture.

Challenging negative thoughts is like holding a magnifying glass up to your fears, examining them closely to see if they hold up under scrutiny. It's about questioning the validity of these thoughts, looking for evidence to support or refute them, and considering alternative explanations.

Here are some strategies you can use to challenge negative thoughts:

1. **Examine the evidence:** What evidence do you have to support this thought? Is it based on facts or feelings? Are there any other ways of interpreting the situation?
2. **Consider the worst-case scenario:** What's the worst that could happen? Is it really as bad as you imagine? What are the chances of it actually happening?
3. **Look for alternative explanations:** Are there other possible explanations for this situation? Could there be a more positive or neutral interpretation?
4. **Challenge your assumptions:** Are you making any assumptions about yourself, others, or the situation? Are these assumptions accurate or helpful?
5. **Reframe your thoughts:** Can you reframe this thought in a more positive or realistic way? For example, instead of thinking "I'm going to fail this test," you could think "I'm going to do my best and learn from the experience, regardless of the outcome."

Once you've challenged your negative thoughts, it's time to replace them with more positive, empowering beliefs. This is like planting new seeds in your mental garden, nurturing them with positive affirmations and realistic expectations.

Here are some tips for replacing negative thoughts:

1. **Focus on your strengths:** Remind yourself of your past successes and the qualities that make you strong and capable.
2. **Practice gratitude:** Take a few moments each day to appreciate the good things in your life, no matter how

small.

3. **Use positive affirmations:** Repeat positive statements to yourself, such as "I am strong," "I am capable," or "I am worthy of love and happiness."
4. **Visualize success:** Imagine yourself achieving your goals and overcoming your challenges.
5. **Surround yourself with positive people:** Spend time with people who uplift and support you, and avoid those who bring you down.

Remember, challenging and replacing negative thoughts takes time and practice. It's a process of learning to recognize your anxious thoughts, question their validity, and choose more positive, empowering beliefs. But with patience and persistence, you can rewire your brain and create a more positive, optimistic outlook on life.

RELAXATION TECHNIQUES

Progressive Muscle Relaxation

Imagine your body as a tightly wound spring, each muscle coiled with tension and stress. This is the reality for many people living with anxiety, their bodies constantly on high alert, braced for the next perceived threat. But what if you could uncoil that spring, releasing the tension and restoring a sense of calm and ease?

Progressive muscle relaxation (PMR) is a powerful technique for achieving just that. It's a guided relaxation exercise that involves systematically tensing and relaxing different muscle groups in your body. Think of it as a gentle massage for your mind and body, melting away stress and promoting deep relaxation.

The idea behind PMR is simple: By tensing your muscles, you bring awareness to the areas where you're holding tension. Then, by consciously relaxing those muscles, you release the pent-up stress and create a sense of physical and mental calm.

Here's how it works:

1. **Find a quiet place:** Choose a comfortable spot where you won't be disturbed. Lie down or sit in a reclined position. Close your eyes or soften your gaze.
2. **Focus on your breath:** Take a few deep breaths, inhaling slowly through your nose and exhaling through your mouth. Feel your body begin to relax with each breath.
3. **Start with your feet:** Tense the muscles in your feet, curling your toes tightly. Hold for a few seconds, noticing the tension in your feet. Then, release the tension, allowing your feet to relax completely.
4. **Move up your body:** Gradually work your way up your body, tensing and relaxing each muscle group in

turn. Tense your calves, thighs, buttocks, stomach, back, chest, shoulders, arms, hands, neck, and face.

5. **Notice the difference:** As you tense and relax each muscle group, pay attention to the difference between tension and relaxation. Notice how it feels to let go of the tension and allow your muscles to soften.

6. **Scan your body:** Once you've relaxed all of your muscle groups, take a moment to scan your body for any remaining tension. If you find any, gently tense and relax those muscles again.

You can practice PMR for as little as 5 minutes or as long as 20 minutes. The key is to be consistent with your practice, ideally doing it once or twice a day.

As you become more familiar with PMR, you can tailor it to your own needs. You can focus on specific muscle groups that tend to hold tension, or you can practice it while sitting at your desk or even lying in bed before you fall asleep.

With regular practice, PMR can help you reduce muscle tension, improve sleep quality, and lower your overall stress levels. It can also help you become more aware of your body and the sensations of tension and relaxation, making it easier to identify and manage anxiety in the moment.

Guided Imagery for Relaxation

Imagine yourself on a warm, sandy beach. The sun kisses your skin as a gentle breeze whispers through your hair. You hear the rhythmic crash of waves against the shore and the distant cries of seagulls soaring overhead. The scent of salty air fills your nostrils, and you feel a profound sense of peace and tranquility washing over you.

This isn't just a daydream – it's a powerful relaxation technique called guided imagery. It's a form of meditation that involves using your imagination to create calming and peaceful scenes in your mind. By immersing yourself in these imaginary scenarios, you can transport yourself away from the stresses of daily life and tap into a deep well of relaxation.

Guided imagery is like a mental vacation, a way to escape the hustle and bustle of your everyday routine and find solace in a tranquil oasis. It's a tool you can use to reduce stress, improve mood, and promote restful sleep.

The beauty of guided imagery is its versatility. You can tailor it to your own preferences, creating scenes that resonate with you personally. Whether you envision yourself strolling through a lush forest, floating in a calm lake, or simply relaxing in your favorite armchair, the key is to create a mental image that evokes feelings of peace and serenity.

Here's how you can practice guided imagery:

1. **Find a quiet place:** Choose a comfortable spot where you won't be disturbed. Lie down or sit in a reclined position. Close your eyes or soften your gaze.
2. **Focus on your breath:** Take a few deep breaths, inhaling slowly through your nose and exhaling through your mouth. Feel your body begin to relax with each breath.
3. **Create your scene:** Imagine yourself in a peaceful and relaxing setting. Engage all of your senses – what do you see, hear, smell, taste, and touch?
4. **Explore your scene:** Allow yourself to wander through your imaginary world, noticing the details and savoring the sensations. Let go of any worries or concerns, and simply be present in the moment.
5. **Return to the present:** When you're ready, gently bring your attention back to your breath and the sensations in your body. Open your eyes and take a moment to appreciate the feeling of calm and relaxation.

You can practice guided imagery for as little as 5 minutes or as long as 30 minutes. The key is to find a duration that works for you and to be consistent with your practice.

If you're new to guided imagery, you can find many guided meditations online or through apps. These recordings can help you visualize relaxing scenes and guide you through the process of relaxation.

With regular practice, guided imagery can become a powerful tool for managing anxiety. It can help you reduce stress, improve sleep quality, and cultivate a sense of inner peace. It's a simple yet effective way to tap into the power of your imagination and create a more peaceful and relaxed state of mind.

SELF-CARE FOR ANXIETY

The Importance of Self-Care

Imagine you're a car. You wouldn't expect to run smoothly without regular maintenance, right? You'd need oil changes, tire rotations, and the occasional tune-up to keep the engine purring. Well, your mind and body are no different. They too need regular care and attention to function optimally, especially when dealing with the added strain of anxiety.

Self-care isn't just about bubble baths and face masks (though those can be lovely!). It's about prioritizing your well-being, both physically and mentally. It's about recognizing that you deserve to be cared for and making a conscious effort to meet your own needs.

Think of self-care as a toolbox filled with essential tools for maintaining your mental and emotional health. It's not a luxury; it's a necessity. Just like you wouldn't neglect your car's maintenance, you shouldn't neglect your own self-care.

When you're struggling with anxiety, self-care becomes even more crucial. Anxiety can deplete your energy, leaving you feeling drained and overwhelmed. It can also lead to unhealthy coping mechanisms, such as overeating, excessive alcohol consumption, or isolating yourself from others.

Self-care is the antidote to these negative patterns. It's about replenishing your energy, nourishing your body and mind, and building resilience to stress. It's about creating a buffer against anxiety, so you can face life's challenges with greater ease and grace.

But self-care isn't just about preventing burnout. It's also about cultivating joy, connection, and meaning in your life. It's about doing things that make you feel good, that bring you peace and fulfillment. It's about nurturing your passions, connecting with loved ones, and finding activities that spark your creativity and curiosity.

Self-care is an act of self-love. It's about recognizing your worth and treating yourself with kindness and compassion. It's about giving yourself permission to rest, to recharge, and to prioritize your own well-being.

So, the next time you feel overwhelmed by anxiety, remember that you have a powerful tool at your disposal: self-care. By taking care of yourself, you're not only managing your anxiety, you're also investing in your long-term health and happiness.

In the next sub-chapter, we'll explore some specific self-care practices that can help you reduce anxiety and improve your overall well-being.

Self-Care Practices for Anxiety

Think of self-care as your personal recipe for well-being, a blend of ingredients that nourish your body, mind, and soul. It's not a one-size-fits-all formula; it's a unique concoction tailored to your individual needs and preferences. The key is to experiment, discover what works for you, and make self-care a regular part of your routine.

Here are some self-care practices that can help you manage anxiety and improve your overall well-being:

Physical Self-Care:

- **Nourish your body:** Eat a balanced diet rich in fruits, vegetables, and whole grains. Avoid processed foods, sugary drinks, and excessive caffeine, which can exacerbate anxiety.
- **Move your body:** Exercise is a natural stress reliever and mood booster. Find an activity you enjoy, whether it's

dancing, swimming, hiking, or simply taking a brisk walk in the park.

- **Prioritize sleep:** Aim for 7-8 hours of quality sleep each night. Establish a relaxing bedtime routine, avoid screens before bed, and create a sleep-conducive environment.
- **Relax your muscles:** Take warm baths, get massages, or practice progressive muscle relaxation to release tension and promote relaxation.

Emotional Self-Care:

- **Practice mindfulness:** Engage in mindfulness meditation or other mindfulness exercises to cultivate awareness and acceptance of your thoughts and feelings.
- **Connect with others:** Spend time with loved ones, join a support group, or talk to a therapist to build a strong support network.
- **Express your emotions:** Don't bottle up your feelings. Write in a journal, talk to a trusted friend, or express yourself through art or music.
- **Set boundaries:** Learn to say no to requests that drain your energy or don't align with your values.
- **Do things you enjoy:** Make time for hobbies, activities, or interests that bring you joy and fulfillment.

Mental Self-Care:

- **Challenge negative thoughts:** Practice cognitive restructuring to identify and challenge negative thought patterns.
- **Learn relaxation techniques:** Explore breathing exercises, guided imagery, or meditation to reduce stress and promote relaxation.
- **Read uplifting books or articles:** Fill your mind with positive and inspiring content.
- **Limit news and social media consumption:** Constant exposure to negative news and social media can fuel anxiety.
- **Engage in activities that challenge your mind:** Learn a new

skill, take a class, or read a book on a topic that interests you.

Spiritual Self-Care:

- **Spend time in nature:** Connect with the natural world to find peace and tranquility.
- **Practice gratitude:** Focus on the things you're grateful for, big and small.
- **Meditate or pray:** Engage in spiritual practices that bring you comfort and meaning.
- **Volunteer your time:** Helping others can boost your mood and give you a sense of purpose.
- **Reflect on your values:** Connect with your inner values and live in alignment with them.

Remember, self-care isn't selfish. It's an essential part of maintaining your mental and emotional well-being. By making self-care a priority, you're investing in your long-term health and happiness.

DIET AND EXERCISE

The Link Between Food and Mood

Imagine your body as a high-performance sports car. You wouldn't fill its tank with sugary drinks and processed snacks, would you? You'd want to give it the best fuel possible to ensure it runs smoothly and efficiently. Well, your brain is no different. It too needs premium fuel to function at its best, especially when dealing with the added strain of anxiety.

The food you eat has a profound impact on your mood, energy levels, and overall well-being. It's not just about calories and nutrients; it's about the complex relationship between your gut and your brain, a connection known as the gut-brain axis.

Think of your gut as a second brain, a vast network of neurons and microorganisms that communicate with your brain via the vagus nerve. This communication highway is a two-way street, with signals traveling back and forth, influencing everything from your mood and emotions to your stress response and immune function.

When you eat a healthy, balanced diet, you're not just nourishing your body; you're also feeding the beneficial bacteria in your gut. These bacteria, known as probiotics, play a crucial role in maintaining a healthy gut microbiome, which in turn has been linked to improved mood, reduced anxiety, and better cognitive function.

On the other hand, a diet high in processed foods, sugar, and unhealthy fats can disrupt the balance of your gut microbiome, leading to inflammation and an increased risk of anxiety and depression. It's like filling your sports car with low-grade fuel – it might still run, but it won't perform at its peak.

Sugar, in particular, is a major culprit when it comes to mood swings and anxiety. It can cause rapid spikes and crashes in blood sugar levels, leading to irritability, fatigue, and difficulty concentrating. Think of it as a roller coaster ride for your brain, with each peak and valley triggering a wave of anxiety.

But it's not just about avoiding the bad stuff. Certain foods can actively promote good mood and reduce anxiety. Foods rich in omega-3 fatty acids, such as salmon, walnuts, and flaxseeds, have been shown to have anti-inflammatory effects and may help reduce symptoms of anxiety and depression.

Complex carbohydrates, like those found in whole grains, fruits, and vegetables, provide a slow and steady release of energy, helping to stabilize blood sugar levels and mood. And protein-rich foods, such as lean meats, fish, eggs, and beans, provide the building blocks for neurotransmitters like serotonin and dopamine, which play a key role in regulating mood.

By making conscious choices about what you eat, you can nourish your gut, support your brain, and create a solid foundation for mental and emotional well-being.

Exercise for Anxiety Relief

Imagine your anxiety as a tightly wound rubber band, stretched to its limit and ready to snap. Now, picture exercise as a pair of gentle hands, slowly unwinding that rubber band, releasing the tension and restoring its elasticity.

Exercise isn't just about building muscle and burning calories. It's a powerful tool for managing anxiety, a natural antidepressant and mood booster that can transform your mental and emotional state.

But how does exercise work its magic on anxiety? It all comes down to a fascinating interplay of brain chemistry, stress hormones, and feel-good neurotransmitters.

When you exercise, your body releases endorphins, natural painkillers and mood elevators that can create a sense of euphoria and well-being. It's that "runner's high" feeling, a rush of energy and positivity that can wash away anxiety and leave you feeling calmer and more focused.

Exercise also helps to reduce levels of cortisol, the stress hormone that can wreak havoc on your body and mind. By lowering cortisol, exercise can help to calm your nervous system, improve sleep quality, and boost your immune function.

But it's not just about the immediate effects. Regular exercise can also create lasting changes in your brain, increasing the production of serotonin and dopamine, neurotransmitters that play a key role in regulating mood and anxiety. Think of it as building a stronger foundation for mental and emotional well-being, one workout at a time.

And the benefits don't stop there. Exercise can also improve your self-esteem, increase your energy levels, and enhance your overall sense of well-being. It can help you feel more confident, capable, and in control of your life.

The beauty of exercise is its versatility. There's no one-size-fits-all approach. You can find an activity that you enjoy and that fits your lifestyle. Whether it's dancing, swimming, hiking, yoga, or simply taking a brisk walk in the park, the key is to move your body and get your heart pumping.

If you're new to exercise, start slowly and gradually increase the intensity and duration of your workouts. Aim for at least 30 minutes of moderate-intensity exercise most days of the week. And remember, consistency is key. The more you exercise, the greater the benefits you'll reap.

So, the next time you feel anxiety creeping in, lace up your sneakers and hit the pavement. Let your body be your therapist, your gym your sanctuary, and your workout your prescription for a happier, healthier you.

SLEEP HYGIENE

The Importance of Sleep for Anxiety

Imagine your mind as a computer. During the day, it's constantly running programs, processing information, and juggling multiple tasks. But at night, it needs time to shut down, defragment, and recharge. Sleep is that essential reboot for your brain, a time for it to repair and restore itself, consolidate memories, and process emotions.

But when anxiety is in the picture, sleep can become elusive. Your mind races with worries, your body tenses up, and you toss and turn for hours, unable to find restful slumber. This sleep deprivation only exacerbates anxiety, creating a vicious cycle of sleepless nights and heightened anxiety.

Think of it like a battery. When you're well-rested, your battery is fully charged, giving you the energy and resilience to cope with life's challenges. But when you're sleep-deprived, your battery is running low, leaving you vulnerable to stress, irritability, and anxiety.

Sleep deprivation affects your brain in profound ways. It impairs your cognitive function, making it harder to concentrate, remember things, and make decisions. It also disrupts your emotional regulation, making you more reactive to stress and more prone to anxiety and depression.

In fact, studies have shown a strong link between sleep deprivation and anxiety disorders. People with insomnia are more likely to develop anxiety disorders, and people with anxiety disorders are more likely to experience insomnia. It's a chicken-and-egg situation, with each condition fueling the other.

But sleep isn't just about quantity; it's also about quality. Deep, restorative sleep is essential for mental and emotional well-being. It's during these deep sleep stages that your brain processes emotions, consolidates memories, and releases growth hormone, which is important for cell repair and regeneration.

When you're sleep-deprived, you miss out on these crucial stages of sleep, leaving you feeling groggy, irritable, and emotionally vulnerable. It's like trying to run a marathon on an empty stomach – you might be able to keep going for a while, but eventually, you'll hit a wall.

So, the next time you find yourself tossing and turning, remember that sleep isn't a luxury; it's a necessity. By prioritizing sleep, you're not only improving your physical health, you're also protecting your mental and emotional well-being.

In the next sub-chapter, we'll explore some practical tips for improving your sleep hygiene and getting the rest you need to manage anxiety and thrive.

Tips for Improving Sleep Quality

Imagine your bedroom as a sanctuary, a haven of peace and tranquility where you can escape the stresses of the day and recharge your batteries. It's a place where you can let go of your worries, drift off to sleep, and wake up feeling refreshed and renewed.

But creating this sleep sanctuary takes more than just a comfortable bed and fluffy pillows. It requires a commitment to good sleep hygiene, a set of habits and practices that promote restful sleep.

Think of sleep hygiene as a recipe for a good night's rest, a blend of ingredients that create the perfect conditions for sleep. By following these tips, you can improve your sleep quality, reduce anxiety, and wake up feeling energized and ready to tackle the day.

Here are some tips for improving your sleep hygiene:

1. **Establish a consistent sleep schedule:** Go to bed and wake up at the same time each day, even on weekends. This helps regulate your body's natural sleep-wake cycle and makes it easier to fall asleep and wake up feeling refreshed.

2. **Create a relaxing bedtime routine:** Wind down before bed with calming activities, such as reading, taking a warm bath, or listening to soothing music. Avoid screens for at least an hour before bed, as the blue light emitted from electronic devices can interfere with sleep.

3. **Make your bedroom sleep-friendly:** Keep your bedroom cool, dark, and quiet. Invest in comfortable bedding and pillows, and consider using blackout curtains or earplugs if needed.

4. **Avoid caffeine and alcohol before bed:** Caffeine can interfere with sleep, even if consumed hours before bedtime. Alcohol may help you fall asleep initially, but it can disrupt your sleep later in the night.

5. **Manage stress and anxiety:** Practice relaxation techniques, such as deep breathing, meditation, or progressive muscle relaxation, to calm your mind and body before bed.

6. **Exercise regularly:** Regular exercise can improve sleep quality, but avoid exercising too close to bedtime, as it can increase alertness and make it harder to fall asleep.

7. **Limit naps:** If you need to nap, keep it short (20-30 minutes) and avoid napping late in the afternoon.

8. **See a doctor if sleep problems persist:** If you're struggling with chronic insomnia or other sleep problems, talk to your doctor. They can help you identify the underlying cause and recommend appropriate treatment.

By making sleep a priority and practicing good sleep hygiene, you can improve your overall health and well-being, reduce anxiety, and wake up each morning feeling refreshed and ready to take on the day.

Remember, sleep is not a luxury; it's a necessity. By investing in your sleep, you're investing in your mental and emotional health.

SOCIAL SUPPORT

The Power of Connection

Imagine you're a lone wolf, howling into the vast wilderness. You're strong and independent, but there's a nagging sense of isolation, a longing for companionship. Humans, like wolves, are social creatures, wired for connection and belonging. And when anxiety strikes, that need for connection becomes even more crucial.

Think of social support as a warm embrace on a cold day, a comforting presence that reminds you that you're not alone. It's a lifeline, a safety net that catches you when you fall and helps you get back on your feet.

When you're struggling with anxiety, it's easy to withdraw from others, to isolate yourself in a cocoon of fear and worry. But this isolation can be a dangerous trap, amplifying your anxiety and leaving you feeling even more alone.

Social connection, on the other hand, is a powerful antidote to anxiety. It's a reminder that you're part of a community, that there are people who care about you and want to support you. It's a source of comfort, encouragement, and perspective, helping you to see beyond your own fears and anxieties.

The power of connection lies in its ability to reduce stress, boost mood, and enhance resilience. Studies have shown that people with strong social support networks are less likely to experience anxiety and depression, and more likely to recover from illness and trauma.

Think of your social support network as a team of cheerleaders, rooting for you and reminding you of your strengths. It's a group of people who can offer a listening ear, a shoulder to cry on, or a helping hand. They can provide practical support, emotional support, or simply a distraction from your worries.

Social support can come in many forms. It could be a close friend, a family member, a therapist, a support group, or even a pet. The key is to have people in your life who you can turn to when you're struggling, who will listen without judgment and offer support and encouragement.

But social connection isn't just about receiving support; it's also about giving it. Reaching out to others, offering a helping hand, or simply sharing a laugh can boost your mood and strengthen your sense of connection. It's a reminder that you're not just a recipient of support, but also a valuable member of a community.

So, the next time you feel anxiety creeping in, don't isolate yourself. Reach out to a friend, join a support group, or volunteer your time. Remember, you're not alone in this. There are people who care about you and want to help. And by connecting with others, you're not only managing your anxiety, you're also enriching your life and strengthening your community.

Building a Strong Support Network

Imagine your social support network as a sturdy bridge, connecting you to others and providing a safe passage through life's storms. It's a bridge built on trust, mutual respect, and shared experiences. And just like any bridge, it requires maintenance and care to ensure it remains strong and stable.

Building a strong support network isn't about amassing a large number of acquaintances. It's about cultivating meaningful relationships with people who genuinely care about your well-being. It's about finding your tribe, a group of individuals who understand you, support you, and challenge you to grow.

Think of it as building a team, each member bringing their unique strengths and perspectives to the table. Some may be great listeners, offering a compassionate ear and a shoulder to cry on. Others may be skilled problem solvers, offering practical advice and solutions. And still others may be simply fun-loving companions, providing a much-needed distraction from your worries.

Here are some tips for building a strong support network:

1. **Be proactive:** Don't wait for others to reach out to you. Take the initiative to connect with people, whether it's inviting a friend for coffee, joining a club or group, or volunteering your time.
2. **Be open and vulnerable:** Share your thoughts and feelings with others, even if it feels uncomfortable. Vulnerability can be a powerful way to build trust and deepen connections.
3. **Be a good listener:** Show genuine interest in others' lives and offer support when needed. Remember, relationships are a two-way street.
4. **Be selective:** Surround yourself with positive and supportive people who lift you up, not drag you down. Don't be afraid to distance yourself from toxic relationships.
5. **Be patient:** Building strong relationships takes time and effort. Don't get discouraged if you don't see results overnight. Keep investing in your relationships, and over time, you'll see your support network grow and strengthen.

Remember, your support network isn't just about helping you through tough times. It's also about celebrating your successes, sharing your joys, and growing together. It's about creating a community of support that enriches your life and helps you thrive.

So, take a moment to reflect on your current support network. Are there areas where you could strengthen it? Are there people you could reach out to, or activities you could join to expand your social circle? By actively building and nurturing your support network, you're not only managing your anxiety, you're also creating a richer, more fulfilling life.

JOURNALING FOR ANXIETY

The Benefits of Journaling

Imagine your mind as a bustling city, thoughts and emotions zipping by like cars on a freeway. Sometimes, it's a smooth ride, but other times, it's a chaotic traffic jam of worries, fears, and anxieties. Journaling is like creating a detour, a quiet side street where you can pull over, take a deep breath, and make sense of the chaos.

Journaling isn't just about recording the events of your day; it's about exploring your inner landscape, unpacking your emotions, and gaining insights into your thoughts and feelings. It's a safe space where you can express yourself without fear of judgment, a blank canvas where you can paint your innermost thoughts and feelings.

Think of your journal as a trusted confidant, a silent listener who never interrupts or offers unsolicited advice. It's a place where you can be completely honest with yourself, where you can vent your frustrations, celebrate your victories, and process your pain.

The benefits of journaling for anxiety are numerous and profound. It can help you:

- **Gain clarity:** By writing down your thoughts and feelings, you can gain a clearer understanding of what's causing your anxiety. You can identify patterns, triggers, and underlying beliefs that may be fueling your fears.
- **Reduce stress:** Journaling can be a cathartic experience, allowing you to release pent-up emotions and anxieties. It can help you to feel lighter, calmer, and more in control.
- **Improve mood:** Expressing your gratitude and focusing on the positive aspects of your life can boost your mood and

reduce feelings of anxiety and depression.

- **Increase self-awareness:** Journaling can help you to become more aware of your thoughts, feelings, and behaviors. This self-awareness can empower you to make positive changes in your life.
- **Problem-solve:** By writing about your challenges and exploring different solutions, you can gain new perspectives and insights.
- **Track your progress:** Journaling can be a way to track your journey with anxiety, noting your successes and challenges along the way. This can help you to stay motivated and see how far you've come.

But journaling isn't just about solving problems or analyzing your emotions. It can also be a source of creativity and self-expression. You can use your journal to write poetry, draw, or simply doodle. You can experiment with different styles and formats, finding what works best for you.

Remember, there are no rules when it comes to journaling. It's your personal space to express yourself freely and honestly. So, grab a pen and paper, or open up a blank document on your computer, and start writing. Let your thoughts and feelings flow onto the page, and see what insights and discoveries emerge.

Journaling Prompts for Anxiety

Imagine your journal as a blank canvas, a safe haven where you can pour out your thoughts and emotions without fear of judgment or criticism. It's a place where you can explore your anxieties, fears, and hopes, and gain a deeper understanding of yourself.

Journaling prompts are like paintbrushes, each one offering a different stroke, a new perspective, a way to delve into the depths of your inner world. They're invitations to explore your emotions, challenge your negative thoughts, and cultivate a sense of gratitude and resilience.

Think of these prompts as stepping stones, guiding you across the river of your anxiety. They can help you uncover hidden patterns, identify triggers, and develop coping strategies. They can also spark creativity, inspire self-reflection, and foster a sense of connection with yourself.

Here are some journaling prompts to get you started:

- **What am I feeling anxious about right now?** Describe your anxiety in detail. What are the physical sensations? What thoughts are running through your mind?
- **What are some of my typical anxiety triggers?** Identify situations, events, or thoughts that tend to trigger your anxiety. Are there any patterns or themes?
- **What negative thoughts or beliefs are contributing to my anxiety?** Explore the negative self-talk that fuels your anxiety. Are there any recurring themes or patterns?
- **What are some healthy coping mechanisms I can use to manage my anxiety?** Brainstorm a list of strategies you can use to cope with anxiety, such as deep breathing, exercise, or mindfulness.
- **What are some things I'm grateful for today?** Take a moment to appreciate the good things in your life, no matter how small. This can help shift your focus from anxiety to gratitude.
- **What is one small step I can take today to reduce my anxiety?** Identify a specific action you can take, such as going for a walk, talking to a friend, or practicing relaxation techniques.

Feel free to use these prompts as a springboard or come up with your own questions to explore. Remember, the most important thing is to be honest and open with yourself in your journaling.

Here are a few additional tips for journaling for anxiety:

- **Set aside dedicated time:** Make journaling a regular part of your routine, even if it's just for a few minutes each day.

- **Write freely:** Don't worry about grammar, spelling, or punctuation. Just let your thoughts flow onto the page.
- **Be kind to yourself:** Don't judge or criticize yourself for your thoughts and feelings. Remember, your journal is a safe space for self-expression.
- **Experiment with different formats:** Try writing in a stream-of-consciousness style, making lists, or even drawing or doodling.

Journaling can be a powerful tool for managing anxiety and promoting mental and emotional well-being. By exploring your inner world and expressing yourself creatively, you can gain valuable insights, develop coping skills, and cultivate a greater sense of peace and self-acceptance.

MANAGING ANXIETY IN THE MOMENT

Grounding Techniques

Imagine you're a kite, soaring high in the sky. The wind whips around you, threatening to carry you away. Anxiety is that wind, a powerful force that can lift you out of the present moment and into a whirlwind of worry and fear. But you have a lifeline: grounding techniques. These simple practices are like anchors, tethering you to the earth and helping you regain your sense of stability.

Grounding techniques are tools you can use to bring yourself back to the present moment when anxiety starts to take over. They're designed to engage your senses, redirect your focus, and anchor you in the here and now. Think of them as a parachute, gently lowering you back to earth when you're caught in a storm of anxiety.

Here are a few grounding techniques you can try:

1. **5-4-3-2-1 Technique:**
   - Name **five** things you can see around you.
   - Name **four** things you can touch.
   - Name **three** things you can hear.
   - Name **two** things you can smell.
   - Name **one** thing you can taste.

This exercise helps you reconnect with your senses and the physical world around you, pulling you away from the spiraling thoughts that fuel anxiety.

2. **Mental Grounding:**

- ○ Recite a poem, song lyrics, or a favorite quote from memory.
- ○ Count backward from 100 by sevens.
- ○ Name all the capitals of the United States (or any other country).

These mental exercises require focus and concentration, drawing your attention away from anxious thoughts and into the present moment.

3. **Physical Grounding:**
- ○ Hold a cool object, like a smooth stone or a piece of ice.
- ○ Run your hands under cold water or splash your face with cold water.
- ○ Focus on the feeling of your feet on the ground.
- ○ Stomp your feet or jump up and down.

These physical sensations can help to anchor you in the present moment and distract you from anxious thoughts.

4. **Soothing Grounding:**
- ○ Wrap yourself in a warm blanket.
- ○ Listen to calming music or nature sounds.
- ○ Sip on a warm beverage, like herbal tea or hot chocolate.

These comforting activities can help to soothe your nervous system and create a sense of safety and security.

The beauty of grounding techniques is their simplicity. You can practice them anywhere, anytime, without any special equipment or training. All you need is a willingness to try something new and a commitment to taking care of yourself in the moment.

Remember, anxiety is like a wave. It may rise and fall, but it will eventually pass. By grounding yourself in the present moment, you can ride out the wave and emerge stronger on the other side.

Coping with Panic Attacks

Imagine you're on a roller coaster, hurtling through twists and turns at breakneck speed. Your heart pounds, your stomach churns, and your breath comes in ragged gasps. You feel a surge of terror, a desperate urge to escape. This is what a panic attack can feel like, an intense wave of fear that can sweep you off your feet and leave you feeling helpless and alone.

Panic attacks are like emotional earthquakes, shaking you to your core and leaving you feeling disoriented and overwhelmed. But even in the midst of this chaos, there are things you can do to ride out the storm and regain your sense of control.

Coping with a panic attack is like navigating a turbulent sea. It requires a combination of grounding techniques, calming strategies, and self-compassion. Here are some tips to help you weather the storm:

1. **Acknowledge the Panic:** The first step is to recognize that you're having a panic attack. Don't try to fight it or deny it. Accept that it's happening and remind yourself that it will pass.
2. **Ground Yourself:** Use the grounding techniques we discussed in the previous section to anchor yourself in the present moment. Focus on your senses, count backward, or recite a familiar phrase.
3. **Breathe Deeply:** Take slow, deep breaths, inhaling through your nose and exhaling through your mouth. Focus on the sensation of your breath entering and leaving your body. This can help to slow your heart rate and calm your nervous system.
4. **Challenge Negative Thoughts:** Panic attacks are often accompanied by catastrophic thoughts, such as "I'm going to die" or "I'm losing control." Remind yourself that these thoughts are not reality. They're just symptoms of anxiety, and they will pass.
5. **Practice Self-Compassion:** Be kind to yourself during a panic attack. Don't judge yourself for feeling anxious. Remind yourself that you're not alone, and that many

people experience panic attacks.

Here are some additional tips that may be helpful:

- **Find a safe place:** If possible, move to a quiet, safe place where you can sit or lie down.
- **Talk to someone:** If you're with someone, tell them you're having a panic attack and ask for their support.
- **Use relaxation techniques:** Progressive muscle relaxation, guided imagery, or mindfulness meditation can help to calm your mind and body.
- **Seek professional help:** If you experience frequent panic attacks, talk to your doctor or a mental health professional. They can help you identify the underlying cause of your anxiety and develop a treatment plan.

Remember, panic attacks are not a sign of weakness or failure. They're a common and treatable condition. By learning to cope with panic attacks, you can regain control of your life and live a fuller, more fulfilling life.

ANXIETY AND RELATIONSHIPS

How Anxiety Can Affect Relationships

Imagine your anxiety as a third wheel on a romantic date, an uninvited guest who casts a shadow over your interactions and creates unnecessary tension. It's that nagging voice in your head, whispering doubts and insecurities, making you question your partner's love and your own worthiness.

Anxiety can be a formidable foe in relationships, a silent saboteur that can erode trust, create conflict, and leave you feeling isolated and alone. But it doesn't have to be this way. By understanding how anxiety can affect relationships, you can learn to navigate its challenges and build stronger, more resilient connections.

Anxiety can manifest in relationships in myriad ways. It can make you overly clingy, constantly seeking reassurance from your partner. It can make you overly critical, nitpicking at your partner's flaws and magnifying their mistakes. It can make you withdraw from intimacy, fearing vulnerability and rejection. It can even trigger jealousy and insecurity, leading to accusations and mistrust.

Think of anxiety as a filter, distorting your perception of your partner and your relationship. It can make you see threats where there are none, interpret neutral comments as criticism, and magnify small disagreements into major conflicts.

Anxiety can also affect your communication. It can make it difficult to express your needs and feelings, or to listen to your partner's perspective. It can lead to misunderstandings, misinterpretations, and a breakdown in communication.

But it's not just you who's affected. Your anxiety can also take a toll on your partner. They may feel frustrated, confused, or resentful. They may feel like they're walking on eggshells, unsure of how to support you without triggering your anxiety.

The good news is that anxiety doesn't have to be a relationship dealbreaker. By recognizing how it can affect your interactions and taking steps to manage it, you can build stronger, healthier, and more fulfilling relationships.

Communicating with Loved Ones About Anxiety

Imagine your anxiety as a hidden burden, a weight you carry alone, fearing that sharing it will make you a burden to others. But what if opening up about your anxiety could actually strengthen your relationships, foster deeper understanding, and create a shared space for healing and growth?

Communicating with loved ones about anxiety can be a daunting task, filled with fear of judgment, rejection, or misunderstanding. But it's also a crucial step towards building stronger, more supportive relationships. By sharing your struggles, you're not only lightening your load, you're also inviting others into your world, giving them the opportunity to offer empathy, compassion, and support.

Think of it like building a bridge, one that spans the gap between your inner world and the world of your loved ones. It's a bridge built on honesty, vulnerability, and trust. By opening up about your anxiety, you're laying the foundation for a deeper, more authentic connection.

But how do you start this conversation? It can be helpful to choose a time and place where you feel comfortable and safe. Start by explaining what anxiety is, how it affects you, and what your triggers are. Be honest about your struggles, but also emphasize your strengths and coping mechanisms.

It's important to remember that your loved ones may not fully understand what you're going through. They may have misconceptions about anxiety, or they may not know how to best support you. Be patient and understanding, and be willing to educate them about your experience.

Here are some tips for communicating with loved ones about anxiety:

1. **Choose your words carefully:** Avoid using language that blames or accuses your loved ones. Instead, focus on how your anxiety affects you and what kind of support you need.
2. **Be specific:** Don't just say "I'm anxious." Explain what you're feeling anxious about, what your triggers are, and how it affects your thoughts and behavior.
3. **Be open to feedback:** Ask your loved ones how they're feeling and what they need from you. Listen to their concerns and validate their feelings.
4. **Set boundaries:** Let your loved ones know what kind of support is helpful and what isn't. Don't be afraid to say no to things that make you feel uncomfortable or overwhelmed.
5. **Express your appreciation:** Let your loved ones know how much you appreciate their support and understanding. This can strengthen your bond and encourage them to continue supporting you.

Remember, communication is a two-way street. It's not just about talking; it's also about listening. By opening up to your loved ones about your anxiety, you're not only helping yourself, you're also deepening your relationships and creating a space for mutual understanding and support.

ANXIETY AT WORK

Managing Anxiety in the Workplace

Imagine your workplace as a bustling beehive, buzzing with activity, deadlines, and expectations. It's a place where you're constantly juggling tasks, meeting demands, and striving to perform at your best. But for those grappling with anxiety, the workplace can feel like a minefield, each step fraught with potential triggers and stressors.

Anxiety at work can manifest in various ways. It could be the dread of presentations, the fear of making mistakes, the pressure to meet deadlines, or the worry of not being good enough. This anxiety can creep in like a stealthy shadow, casting a cloud over your workday and affecting your performance, productivity, and overall well-being.

Imagine the anxious thoughts as a relentless soundtrack playing in the background of your workday. They whisper doubts, magnify fears, and chip away at your confidence. They tell you that you're not qualified, that you'll mess up, that your colleagues are judging you, and that your boss is disappointed in you.

These thoughts can trigger a cascade of physical symptoms, such as a racing heart, sweaty palms, and a churning stomach. They can make it difficult to focus, make decisions, and interact with others. In severe cases, they can even lead to panic attacks, making it impossible to function at work.

But anxiety at work doesn't have to be a life sentence. By understanding its causes and developing effective coping strategies, you can learn to manage your anxiety and thrive in your career.

Here are some tips for managing anxiety at work:

1. **Identify your triggers:** What specific aspects of your job trigger your anxiety? Is it public speaking, meetings, deadlines, or interactions with certain colleagues? Once you know your triggers, you can develop strategies to manage them.
2. **Practice relaxation techniques:** Take short breaks throughout the day to practice deep breathing, mindfulness, or progressive muscle relaxation. These techniques can help to calm your nervous system and reduce stress.
3. **Set realistic expectations:** Don't put too much pressure on yourself to be perfect. Remember, everyone makes mistakes. Focus on doing your best and learning from your experiences.
4. **Talk to your supervisor:** If your anxiety is interfering with your work, talk to your supervisor. They may be able to offer support, such as flexible work arrangements or accommodations.
5. **Seek professional help:** If your anxiety is severe or persistent, consider seeking help from a mental health professional. They can teach you coping skills and help you develop a treatment plan.

Remember, you're not alone in this. Many people struggle with anxiety at work. By recognizing the signs, seeking support, and developing coping strategies, you can navigate the workplace with confidence and achieve your career goals.

Setting Boundaries and Saying No

Imagine your workday as a plate, piled high with tasks, responsibilities, and expectations. It's a tempting buffet, but one that can quickly lead to overwhelm and burnout if you're not careful. For those struggling with anxiety, setting boundaries and learning to say no are essential skills for maintaining balance and protecting your well-being.

Think of your boundaries as a protective shield, a force field that deflects unreasonable demands and prevents you from overextending yourself. It's not about being selfish or uncooperative; it's about recognizing your limits and prioritizing your mental and emotional health.

In the workplace, boundaries can take many forms. It could be saying no to taking on additional projects, declining after-work social events, or setting limits on how often you check your email outside of work hours. It could also involve communicating your needs to your colleagues and supervisor, such as needing a quiet space to work or taking breaks to manage your anxiety.

Saying no can be particularly challenging for people with anxiety. We often fear disappointing others, being judged, or losing opportunities. But saying yes to everything can leave you feeling overwhelmed, stressed, and resentful.

Think of saying no as a muscle, one that needs to be exercised and strengthened over time. It's not about being rude or dismissive; it's about communicating your limits in a respectful and assertive way.

Here are some tips for setting boundaries and saying no at work:

1. **Know your limits:** Be honest with yourself about how much you can realistically handle. Don't take on more than you can chew, even if it means saying no to opportunities that seem tempting.
2. **Practice saying no:** It may feel uncomfortable at first, but the more you practice, the easier it will become. Start with small requests and gradually work your way up to bigger ones.
3. **Be assertive:** When saying no, be clear, direct, and concise. Avoid apologizing or making excuses. Simply state your position and offer an alternative solution if possible.

4. **Communicate your needs:** Let your colleagues and supervisor know what you need to be successful at work. This could include flexible work arrangements, breaks to manage anxiety, or a quiet workspace.

5. **Don't overcommit:** Be realistic about your time and energy. Don't schedule back-to-back meetings or overbook your calendar. Leave some buffer time for unexpected tasks or challenges.

Remember, setting boundaries and saying no is not a sign of weakness. It's a sign of self-respect and self-preservation. By prioritizing your well-being, you're not only protecting yourself from burnout, you're also setting a positive example for your colleagues and creating a healthier workplace culture.

ANXIETY AND PARENTING

Parenting with Anxiety

Imagine parenting as a tightrope walk, a delicate balancing act between nurturing your child and managing your own anxieties. It's a beautiful, rewarding journey, but one that can be fraught with challenges, especially when anxiety casts a shadow over your parenting experience.

Parenting with anxiety can feel like a constant battle, a tug-of-war between your desire to be the best parent you can be and the intrusive thoughts and worries that plague your mind. It's a balancing act between meeting your child's needs and tending to your own mental health.

Imagine your anxiety as a whisper in your ear, constantly questioning your decisions, amplifying your fears, and undermining your confidence. It can make you doubt your parenting abilities, second-guess your instincts, and worry excessively about your child's safety and well-being.

Anxiety can manifest in parenting in various ways. It can make you overly protective, constantly hovering over your child and restricting their independence. It can make you overly critical, focusing on your child's mistakes and shortcomings. It can also make you emotionally unavailable, withdrawing from your child due to your own anxiety-related struggles.

Think of anxiety as a filter, distorting your perception of your child and your parenting role. It can make you see threats where there are none, interpret your child's behavior as a reflection of your parenting skills, and magnify minor challenges into major crises.

But anxiety doesn't have to define your parenting experience. By understanding how it can affect your parenting style and developing coping strategies, you can break free from its grip and become the parent you want to be.

Here are some tips for parenting with anxiety:

1. **Acknowledge your anxiety:** Don't try to deny or suppress your anxiety. Recognize that it's a part of you, but it doesn't have to control you.
2. **Practice self-care:** Make time for activities that help you manage your anxiety, such as exercise, relaxation techniques, or therapy.
3. **Set realistic expectations:** Don't strive for perfection. Parenting is a journey of learning and growth, and it's okay to make mistakes along the way.
4. **Focus on the present moment:** Don't get caught up in worries about the future or regrets about the past. Be present with your child and enjoy the precious moments you have together.
5. **Talk to your child about anxiety:** Explain what anxiety is and how it affects you. This can help your child understand your behavior and feel less alone if they experience anxiety themselves.

Remember, you're not alone in this. Many parents struggle with anxiety. By seeking support, developing coping skills, and prioritizing your mental health, you can overcome the challenges of parenting with anxiety and create a loving and nurturing environment for your child.

Helping Anxious Children

Imagine your child as a delicate sapling, swaying in the wind of anxiety. Their little minds are filled with worries, fears, and insecurities, and they look to you, their parent, for guidance and reassurance. As a parent, it's your job to nurture that sapling, to provide a safe and supportive environment where it can grow strong and resilient.

Helping an anxious child can be a challenging but rewarding journey. It requires patience, empathy, and a deep understanding of their unique struggles. It's about teaching them coping skills, empowering them to manage their anxiety, and instilling in them a sense of confidence and self-efficacy.

Think of yourself as a gardener, tending to your child's emotional garden. You can't control the weather or prevent storms from brewing, but you can provide the right soil, water, and sunlight to help your child's resilience blossom.

Anxiety in children can manifest in various ways. They may be clingy, have difficulty sleeping, complain of stomach aches or headaches, or exhibit irritability or anger. They may also have trouble concentrating, performing at school, or making friends.

It's important to remember that anxiety is a normal part of childhood. All children experience anxiety from time to time, especially when facing new challenges or situations. But when anxiety becomes excessive, persistent, and interferes with a child's daily life, it may be a sign of an anxiety disorder.

Here are some tips for helping an anxious child:

1. **Validate their feelings:** Let your child know that it's okay to feel anxious. Don't dismiss their worries or tell them to "just relax." Instead, listen attentively, offer comfort, and validate their emotions.
2. **Teach coping skills:** Help your child develop healthy coping mechanisms, such as deep breathing exercises, mindfulness techniques, or progressive muscle relaxation. Practice these skills together, and encourage your child to use them when they feel anxious.
3. **Encourage open communication:** Create a safe space where your child feels comfortable talking about their anxieties. Let them know that you're there to listen and

support them, without judgment or criticism.

4. **Model healthy coping mechanisms:** Children learn by watching their parents. By modeling healthy ways of coping with stress and anxiety, you're teaching your child valuable life skills.

5. **Seek professional help:** If your child's anxiety is severe or persistent, consider seeking help from a mental health professional. They can provide additional support and guidance, and teach your child coping skills tailored to their specific needs.

Remember, helping an anxious child is a marathon, not a sprint. It takes time, patience, and consistent effort. But by providing love, support, and guidance, you can empower your child to overcome their anxieties and thrive.

SEEKING PROFESSIONAL HELP

When to Seek Professional Help

Imagine you're driving a car that's making a strange noise. At first, it's just a faint rattle, barely noticeable. But over time, it grows louder and more persistent, until it's all you can hear. You try to ignore it, hoping it will go away on its own. But it doesn't. In fact, it seems to be getting worse. You know you should take it to a mechanic, but you're hesitant. You worry about the cost, the inconvenience, and the possibility that something might be seriously wrong.

Anxiety can be like that rattling car. At first, it's just a minor annoyance, a fleeting worry that passes quickly. But over time, it can grow louder and more persistent, interfering with your daily life and causing significant distress. You may try to manage it on your own, hoping it will go away on its own. But it doesn't.

Just like a car needs a mechanic, sometimes anxiety needs a professional. There's no shame in seeking help; in fact, it's a sign of strength and self-awareness. A mental health professional can provide you with the tools and support you need to manage your anxiety and regain control of your life.

But how do you know when it's time to seek professional help? Here are some signs that your anxiety may warrant professional attention:

- **Your anxiety is interfering with your daily life:** If your anxiety is preventing you from going to work, school, or social events, or if it's making it difficult to perform your daily tasks, it's time to seek help.

- **Your anxiety is causing you significant distress:** If you're feeling overwhelmed, hopeless, or like you can't cope, it's important to reach out for support.
- **Your anxiety is accompanied by physical symptoms:** If you're experiencing physical symptoms like chest pain, difficulty breathing, or a racing heart, it's important to see a doctor to rule out any medical causes.
- **You've tried self-help strategies, but they're not working:** If you've tried relaxation techniques, exercise, and other self-care practices, but your anxiety isn't improving, it may be time to seek professional help.
- **You're having thoughts of self-harm or suicide:** If you're experiencing suicidal thoughts or urges to harm yourself, seek help immediately. Call a crisis hotline or go to your nearest emergency room.

Remember, seeking professional help is not a sign of weakness. It's a brave and important step towards healing and recovery. A mental health professional can provide you with the support, guidance, and tools you need to manage your anxiety and live a full and meaningful life.

Different Types of Therapy for Anxiety

Imagine you're standing at a crossroads, unsure of which path to take. Anxiety has been your unwanted companion for far too long, and you're ready to embark on a journey towards healing and recovery. But which route will lead you to the destination of peace and well-being?

Just like a traveler needs a map, seeking professional help for anxiety requires understanding the different types of therapy available. Each therapy is like a different path, offering unique tools and techniques to help you navigate the terrain of your anxiety.

Think of therapy as a toolbox, filled with a variety of instruments designed to address different aspects of your anxiety. Some tools may be more effective than others, depending on your individual needs and preferences. The key is to find the right tools for your journey.

Here are some of the most common types of therapy for anxiety:

1. **Cognitive Behavioral Therapy (CBT):** This approach focuses on identifying and changing negative thought patterns and behaviors that contribute to anxiety. It's like rewiring your brain, replacing the faulty wiring that triggers anxiety with new, healthier connections.

2. **Exposure Therapy:** This involves gradually facing your fears in a safe and controlled environment. It's like slowly dipping your toes into the water, gradually building up your tolerance to the things that trigger your anxiety.

3. **Acceptance and Commitment Therapy (ACT):** This approach teaches you to accept your thoughts and feelings without judgment, and to focus on living a meaningful life in accordance with your values. It's like learning to surf the waves of anxiety, rather than trying to fight against them.

4. **Mindfulness-Based Stress Reduction (MBSR):** This program combines mindfulness meditation with yoga and other relaxation techniques to reduce stress and improve overall well-being. It's like creating a calm oasis in the midst of a storm, a place where you can retreat and recharge.

In addition to these evidence-based therapies, there are also alternative therapies that may be helpful for managing anxiety, such as acupuncture, massage therapy, and herbal remedies.

Choosing the right therapy is like finding the right pair of shoes. It should fit your needs, feel comfortable, and support you on your journey. Don't be afraid to try different approaches until you find one that resonates with you.

Remember, therapy is not a quick fix. It takes time, effort, and commitment. But with the right therapist and the right tools, you can learn to manage your anxiety and live a fuller, more fulfilling life.

64

ALTERNATIVE THERAPIES

Acupuncture and Acupressure

Imagine your body as a vast landscape, crisscrossed with rivers of energy known as qi (pronounced "chee"). These rivers flow through channels called meridians, nourishing your organs and tissues and maintaining balance in your body and mind. But when stress and anxiety disrupt the flow of qi, it's like a dam blocking a river, creating a buildup of tension and disharmony.

Acupuncture and acupressure are ancient Chinese healing practices that aim to restore the flow of qi and promote balance in the body. Think of them as skilled plumbers, using tiny needles or gentle pressure to unclog the channels and allow the energy to flow freely again.

Acupuncture involves inserting thin needles into specific points along the meridians. These points are like access points to the body's energy system, and by stimulating them, acupuncturists can rebalance the flow of qi and alleviate a wide range of ailments, including anxiety.

Acupressure, on the other hand, uses finger pressure instead of needles to stimulate the same points. It's a self-care technique that you can practice at home to relieve stress, reduce anxiety, and promote relaxation.

The science behind acupuncture and acupressure is still being explored, but there's growing evidence to suggest that they can be effective for managing anxiety. Studies have shown that acupuncture can reduce anxiety symptoms, lower stress hormone levels, and improve sleep quality. Acupressure has also been shown to be effective in reducing anxiety, particularly in people with generalized anxiety disorder.

But how does it work? One theory is that acupuncture and acupressure stimulate the release of endorphins, the body's natural painkillers and mood elevators. They may also activate the parasympathetic nervous system, the "rest and digest" branch of the nervous system that promotes relaxation and reduces stress.

Another theory is that acupuncture and acupressure help to regulate the flow of neurotransmitters, such as serotonin and dopamine, which play a key role in mood regulation. By balancing these brain chemicals, acupuncture and acupressure may help to alleviate anxiety and depression.

If you're considering trying acupuncture or acupressure for anxiety, it's important to find a qualified practitioner who has experience treating anxiety disorders. You should also discuss any concerns or questions you have with your doctor before starting treatment.

Remember, acupuncture and acupressure are not a substitute for conventional medical treatment. But they can be a valuable complement to your overall anxiety management plan, offering a natural and holistic approach to healing and well-being.

Herbal Remedies for Anxiety

Imagine stepping into a fragrant apothecary, filled with jars of dried herbs, roots, and flowers. The air is thick with the scent of lavender, chamomile, and lemon balm, each with its unique healing properties. For centuries, people have turned to these natural remedies to soothe their anxieties, calm their minds, and restore balance to their bodies.

Herbal remedies for anxiety are like gentle whispers of nature, offering a soothing balm for frayed nerves and restless minds. They're not a quick fix, but rather a holistic approach to healing that addresses the root causes of anxiety rather than just masking the symptoms.

Think of herbal remedies as allies, working alongside you to restore harmony to your body and mind. They can be taken in various forms, such as teas, tinctures, capsules, or essential oils. Each herb has its own unique properties and benefits, and finding the right one for you may require some experimentation.

Here are some of the most commonly used herbal remedies for anxiety:

- **Lavender:** This fragrant herb has long been prized for its calming and relaxing properties. Studies have shown that lavender can reduce anxiety, improve sleep quality, and even alleviate symptoms of depression.
- **Chamomile:** This gentle herb is often used as a sleep aid, but it can also be helpful for anxiety. Chamomile has been shown to reduce anxiety symptoms, promote relaxation, and even boost the immune system.
- **Lemon balm:** This lemony herb has a long history of use for anxiety and stress. It's been shown to reduce anxiety symptoms, improve mood, and enhance cognitive function.
- **Passionflower:** This exotic flower has been used for centuries to treat anxiety and insomnia. Studies have shown that passionflower can reduce anxiety, improve sleep quality, and even alleviate symptoms of withdrawal from benzodiazepines, a class of anti-anxiety medications.
- **Valerian root:** This pungent root is another popular remedy for anxiety and insomnia. It's been shown to promote relaxation, improve sleep quality, and reduce anxiety symptoms.

It's important to note that herbal remedies are not a substitute for conventional medical treatment. They should be used in conjunction with other therapies, such as counseling, medication, or lifestyle changes. It's also important to consult with a qualified healthcare professional before starting any herbal remedy, especially if you're pregnant, breastfeeding, or taking other medications.

Remember, herbal remedies are like gentle whispers, not megaphones. They work gradually, subtly shifting your body and mind towards a state of greater balance and well-being. By incorporating them into your daily routine, you can tap into the healing power of nature and find relief from anxiety's grip.

BUILDING RESILIENCE

What is Resilience?

Imagine yourself as a sturdy oak tree, deeply rooted in the earth. The wind may howl, the rain may pour, and the storms may rage, but you remain steadfast, bending but not breaking. This is the essence of resilience, the ability to withstand adversity, adapt to change, and bounce back from life's challenges.

Resilience isn't about being invincible or immune to pain and suffering. It's about having the strength and flexibility to navigate life's ups and downs, to learn from setbacks, and to emerge stronger on the other side.

Think of resilience as a muscle, one that can be strengthened through training and practice. It's not something you're born with; it's something you develop over time, through experience and adversity.

Resilient people aren't superhuman. They experience pain, sadness, and fear just like everyone else. But they have a different relationship with these emotions. They don't let them define them or control them. Instead, they view them as opportunities for growth and learning.

Resilience is about bouncing back, not bouncing around. It's not about denying or suppressing your emotions, but about acknowledging them, processing them, and moving forward. It's about finding meaning in adversity, learning from your mistakes, and using your experiences to grow stronger and wiser.

Resilience is a key ingredient in managing anxiety. When you're resilient, you're less likely to be overwhelmed by stress and anxiety, and more likely to bounce back from setbacks. You have a sense of inner strength and confidence that allows you to face challenges head-on, knowing that you have the tools and resources to cope.

But resilience isn't just about coping with adversity; it's also about thriving in the face of it. Resilient people are not only able to withstand challenges, but they're also able to use them as opportunities for growth and transformation. They're able to find meaning in their struggles and use their experiences to become stronger, wiser, and more compassionate.

In the next sub-chapter, we'll explore some strategies for building resilience and cultivating a more positive and empowered mindset.

Building Resilience for Anxiety

Imagine resilience as a toolbox, filled with tools and strategies that can help you weather life's storms. It's not a one-size-fits-all kit; it's a personalized collection of resources that you build and adapt over time. By filling your toolbox with the right tools, you can develop the strength and flexibility to navigate challenges, overcome setbacks, and thrive in the face of adversity.

Think of building resilience as a journey, not a destination. It's a lifelong process of learning, growing, and adapting. Just like a muscle, resilience requires regular exercise to stay strong and flexible. The more you practice resilience, the better equipped you'll be to handle whatever life throws your way.

Here are some strategies you can use to build resilience for anxiety:

1. **Challenge negative thoughts:** Anxiety often feeds on negative thoughts and beliefs. By learning to identify and challenge these thoughts, you can reframe your perspective and cultivate a more positive outlook.
2. **Practice mindfulness:** Mindfulness can help you become more aware of your thoughts and feelings,

allowing you to respond to them in a more balanced and compassionate way.

3. **Develop coping skills:** Learn relaxation techniques, such as deep breathing, meditation, or yoga, to manage stress and anxiety.

4. **Build a strong support network:** Surround yourself with positive and supportive people who can offer encouragement and guidance.

5. **Set realistic goals:** Don't try to do too much at once. Break down your goals into smaller, more manageable steps.

6. **Celebrate your successes:** Acknowledge and celebrate your achievements, no matter how small. This can help boost your confidence and motivation.

7. **Learn from your mistakes:** View setbacks as opportunities for growth and learning. Don't beat yourself up for mistakes; instead, use them as a chance to improve.

8. **Practice self-compassion:** Be kind to yourself when you're struggling. Remember, everyone makes mistakes and experiences setbacks.

9. **Take care of your physical health:** Eat a healthy diet, exercise regularly, and get enough sleep. Taking care of your body can help to reduce stress and anxiety.

10. **Seek professional help:** If you're struggling to manage your anxiety on your own, don't hesitate to seek help from a therapist or counselor. They can provide you with additional support and guidance.

Remember, building resilience takes time and effort. It's not a quick fix, but a lifelong journey of self-discovery and growth. By practicing these strategies, you can develop the strength and flexibility to overcome challenges, manage anxiety, and thrive in the face of adversity.

YOUR PERSONALIZED ANXIETY MANAGEMENT PLAN

Putting it All Together

Imagine your anxiety management plan as a toolbox, filled with a diverse array of tools and techniques, each one carefully selected to address your unique needs and challenges. This isn't a generic, one-size-fits-all solution; it's a personalized roadmap, a customized guide to navigating the terrain of your anxiety and reclaiming your life.

Think of yourself as a skilled craftsperson, carefully assembling a mosaic of strategies, each piece contributing to a beautiful and harmonious whole. It's not about finding a single magic bullet, but about weaving together a tapestry of tools that empower you to manage anxiety and thrive.

Throughout this book, we've explored a wide range of techniques for coping with anxiety, from mindfulness and breathing exercises to cognitive restructuring and self-care practices. Now, it's time to take these individual pieces and create a cohesive and comprehensive plan that works for you.

Start by reflecting on what you've learned. Which techniques resonated with you the most? Which ones did you find most helpful in managing your anxiety? Which ones do you feel most comfortable and confident using?

Next, consider your specific needs and challenges. What are your triggers? What are your most common symptoms? What are your goals for managing your anxiety?

Based on your reflections and insights, start to assemble your personalized anxiety management plan. This might include:

- **Daily practices:** Incorporate mindfulness exercises, breathing techniques, or relaxation exercises into your daily routine.
- **Coping skills:** Develop a repertoire of coping skills that you can use in the moment when anxiety strikes, such as grounding techniques, positive self-talk, or reaching out to a supportive friend.
- **Lifestyle changes:** Make healthy changes to your diet, exercise routine, and sleep habits.
- **Professional support:** Consider seeking therapy or counseling to address the underlying causes of your anxiety and develop additional coping skills.

Remember, your anxiety management plan isn't set in stone. It's a living document that can be adapted and modified as your needs and circumstances change. Experiment with different techniques, track your progress, and adjust your plan as needed.

Think of it as a recipe, one that you can tweak and refine until you find the perfect combination of ingredients that work for you. It's not about following a rigid formula, but about creating a plan that feels authentic and empowering.

By putting it all together, you're not just managing your anxiety, you're taking control of your life. You're creating a roadmap for well-being, a path that leads to greater peace, resilience, and joy.

Staying Motivated and On Track

Imagine you're a marathon runner, poised at the starting line. The road ahead is long and winding, filled with twists, turns, and unexpected challenges. It's easy to feel overwhelmed, to doubt your abilities, to wonder if you have what it takes to reach the finish line. But deep down, you know you're capable, you're determined, and you're ready to take on the challenge.

Managing anxiety is like running a marathon. It's not a sprint, but a long-term commitment to self-care, resilience, and growth. It requires perseverance, dedication, and a willingness to face setbacks and challenges along the way.

But just like a marathon runner needs motivation to keep going, you need motivation to stay on track with your anxiety management plan. It's not always easy, especially when anxiety tries to sabotage your efforts. But with the right mindset and strategies, you can stay motivated, overcome obstacles, and achieve your goals.

Think of motivation as a flame, one that needs to be nurtured and protected to keep it burning brightly. It's not something that comes and goes; it's something you cultivate through conscious effort and positive reinforcement.

Here are some tips for staying motivated and on track with your anxiety management plan:

1. **Set realistic goals:** Don't try to do too much at once. Start with small, achievable goals and gradually increase the challenge as you build confidence and momentum.
2. **Track your progress:** Keep a journal or use a tracking app to monitor your progress and celebrate your successes. Seeing how far you've come can be a powerful motivator.
3. **Reward yourself:** Celebrate your milestones, no matter how small. Treat yourself to something you enjoy, like a massage, a movie night, or a new book.
4. **Find a support system:** Surround yourself with people who understand and support your journey. Join a support group, talk to a therapist, or connect with friends and family who can offer encouragement and accountability.
5. **Don't give up:** Setbacks are a natural part of the process. Don't let them discourage you. Learn from

your mistakes, adjust your approach, and keep moving forward.

6. **Be kind to yourself:** Don't beat yourself up for having a bad day or struggling with anxiety. Remember, you're human, and it's okay to have ups and downs.
7. **Focus on the positive:** Instead of dwelling on your shortcomings, focus on your strengths and accomplishments. Celebrate your resilience and determination.
8. **Practice gratitude:** Take a few moments each day to appreciate the good things in your life, no matter how small. Gratitude can help shift your focus from anxiety to positivity.

Remember, managing anxiety is a journey, not a destination. It's about progress, not perfection. By staying motivated and on track, you can create a life that is less defined by anxiety and more filled with joy, peace, and purpose.

EMBRACING YOUR JOURNEY

Anxiety, much like a shadow, can follow you through life, casting doubts and fears onto your path. But as you've journeyed through this book, you've discovered that you possess the power to reshape that shadow, to transform it into a source of strength and growth.

You've learned that anxiety is not a life sentence, but a challenge that can be met with courage, resilience, and a wealth of tools and strategies. You've explored the intricate connection between your mind and body, delved into the depths of your thoughts and emotions, and discovered the power of self-care, connection, and professional support.

You've learned to identify your triggers, challenge negative thoughts, and cultivate a more positive and empowered mindset. You've embraced the practice of mindfulness, harnessed the calming power of your breath, and discovered the joy of movement and nourishment.

But this book is just the beginning of your journey. It's a starting point, a springboard for continued growth and self-discovery. The tools and techniques you've learned are seeds that you can plant and nurture, allowing them to blossom into a life that is less defined by anxiety and more filled with peace, joy, and fulfillment.

Remember, this is your journey, and you are the author of your own story. There will be challenges along the way, but you are equipped with the knowledge, skills, and resilience to overcome them.

Embrace your anxiety as a teacher, a guide that can show you the path to greater self-awareness, compassion, and strength.

Embrace the journey, for it is in the journey that you will find true healing and transformation.

The road to recovery may be long and winding, but it is a road worth traveling. And as you walk this path, remember that you are not alone. There are countless others who have walked this path before you, and countless others who will walk it after you. We are all in this together, supporting each other, learning from each other, and growing together.

So, take a deep breath, embrace your journey, and step boldly into the future. The life you've always dreamed of is waiting for you on the other side of anxiety.

www.ingramcontent.com/pod-product-compliance
Lightning Source LLC
Chambersburg PA
CBHW051837250726
48659CB00005B/1898